Daryl Cagle's "Hillary Clinton and the Democrats" Coloring Book!
Artwork and text by Daryl Cagle

Published by Cagle Cartoons, Inc.
ISBN-13: 978-0692704776
ISBN-10: 0692704779
Printed in the United States of America, First Printing: May, 2016

Hillary vs. Jeb Bush

Early in the 2016 race, Jeb Bush was the likely Republican nominee and critics complained about a dynasty election between American "royal" families

Heavy Baggage for Hillary

Bernie Sanders did well in the 2016 campaign, and for a while it looked like Hillary might sink under the weight of her "baggage."

Young Women Love Bernie

Bernie Sanders attracted younger voters, especially women, who Hillary's campaign thought should be loyal to Hillary.

BFFFFFFFT

Nails in Bernie's Coffin

Even when Hillary wrapped up all the delegates she needed to win the Democratic nomination, Bernie just wouldn't quite quit.

DARYLCAGLE.com

Democrats' Hearts and Minds

Voters chose Hillary, but without much enthusiasm. Bernie Sanders voters were passionate.

MIND

HEART

DEMOCRATS' HEARTS AND MINDS.

DarylCagle.com PoliticalCartoons.com

Hillary Did the Same Thing as Bernie

In the 2008 presidential race, when Obama clinched up the Democratic nomination, Hillary did the same thing as Bernie, staying in the race because "anything could happen."

Poor Hillary

Hillary complained, when she and Bill left the White House with big legal bills from Bill's impeachment, that she was "flat broke."

DARYL
CAGLE
POLITICALCARTOON.com

Bill Clinton and the Clinton Foundation

After leaving office, Bill Clinton raked in money for his "Clinton Foundation" from countries around the world, leaving Hillary to struggle with how that looks to the media.

Benghazi
Republicans and Fox News are frantic to pin the blame on Hillary.

Hillary and the Tea Party

Republicans and Fox News eagerly try to sink Hillary over her e-mail scandal.

A Storm Over Hillary's E-mail

Criticism over the e-mail scandal comes down hard on Hillary.

DARYL
CAGLE
.COM

Tough Slog

For a time it looked like Hillary's e-mail scandal could hold her back.

Hillary's Benghazi Testimony

Hillary testified for many hours before hostile Republicans in Congress who wanted to pin the blame on Benghazi.

, members of the Committ
s in Benghazi on September 11, 2012
Stevens, Sean Smith, Tyrone Woods, and Glen
nge to the United States and our partners in North
or this challenge and share what we've learned, how we
work together to honor our fallen colleagues and continue
and values.
ear-eyed examination of this matter must begin with this sobering fa
n 19 Accountability Review Boards investigating attacks on American dip
ties. Benghazi joins a long list of tragedies, for our Department and for
ges taken in Tehran in 1979, our embassy and Marine barracks bombed in Beiru
rs in Saudi Arabia in 1996, our embassies in East Africa in 1998, consulate sta
dah in 2004, the Khost attack in 2009, and too many others.
Of course, the list of attacks foiled, crises averted, and lives saved is even lo
ould never forget that our security professionals get it right 99 percent of the ti
fficult odds all over the world. That's why, like my predecessors, I trust them wi
Let's also remember that administrations of both parties, in partnership with Con
ade concerted and good faith efforts to learn from the tragedies that have occurre
ecommendations from the Review Boards, to seek necessary resources, and to better
eople from constantly evolving threats. That's what the men and women who serve
eserve. And it's what we are doing again now, with your help. As Secretary, I
priority, and no greater responsibility.
As I have said many times since September 11, I take responsibility. Nobody is
getting this right. I am determined to leave the State Department and our coun
nd more secure.
Taking responsibility meant moving quickly in those first uncertain hours a
e immediate crisis and further protect our people and posts in high-threat a
ion and the world. It meant launching an independent investigation to dete
pened in Benghazi and to recommend steps for improvement. And it meant in
mbat terrorism and support emerging democracies in North Africa and beyo
me share some of the lessons we have learned, the steps we have taken
to do.
ear-eyed examination of this matter must begin with this soberi
9 Accountability Review Boards investigating attacks on Ame
enghazi joins a long list of tragedies, for our Depa
Tehran in 1979, our embassy and Marine barra
in 1996, our embassies in East A
our embassy and
HILLARY CLINTON
DARYL CAGLE
POLITICALCARTOONS.COM

Hillary's Vote to Invade Iraq

Democrats didn't care about Hillary's e-mail scandal, but they didn't like her vote, in the Senate, to invade Iraq – something both Bernie and Trump bring up at every opportunity.

YOUR IRAQ WAR VOTE?
are YOU SORRY FOR YOUR IRAQ VOTE??
YOUR IRAQ VOTE? ARE YOU SORRY?
IRAQ WAR AUTHORIZATION VOTE?
YOUR WAR VOTE?
WAR VOTE?
IRAQ WAR VOTE?
WAR AUTHORIZATION VOTE?
ARE YOU SORRY SORRY SORRY?
IRAQ VOTE!
SORRY FOR YOUR IRAQ VOTE?
SORRY?
DARYL CAGLE

Most Unpopular Democratic Candidate

Could Hillary be the most unpopular Democratic presidential candidate ever?
Some disappointed Democrats think so.

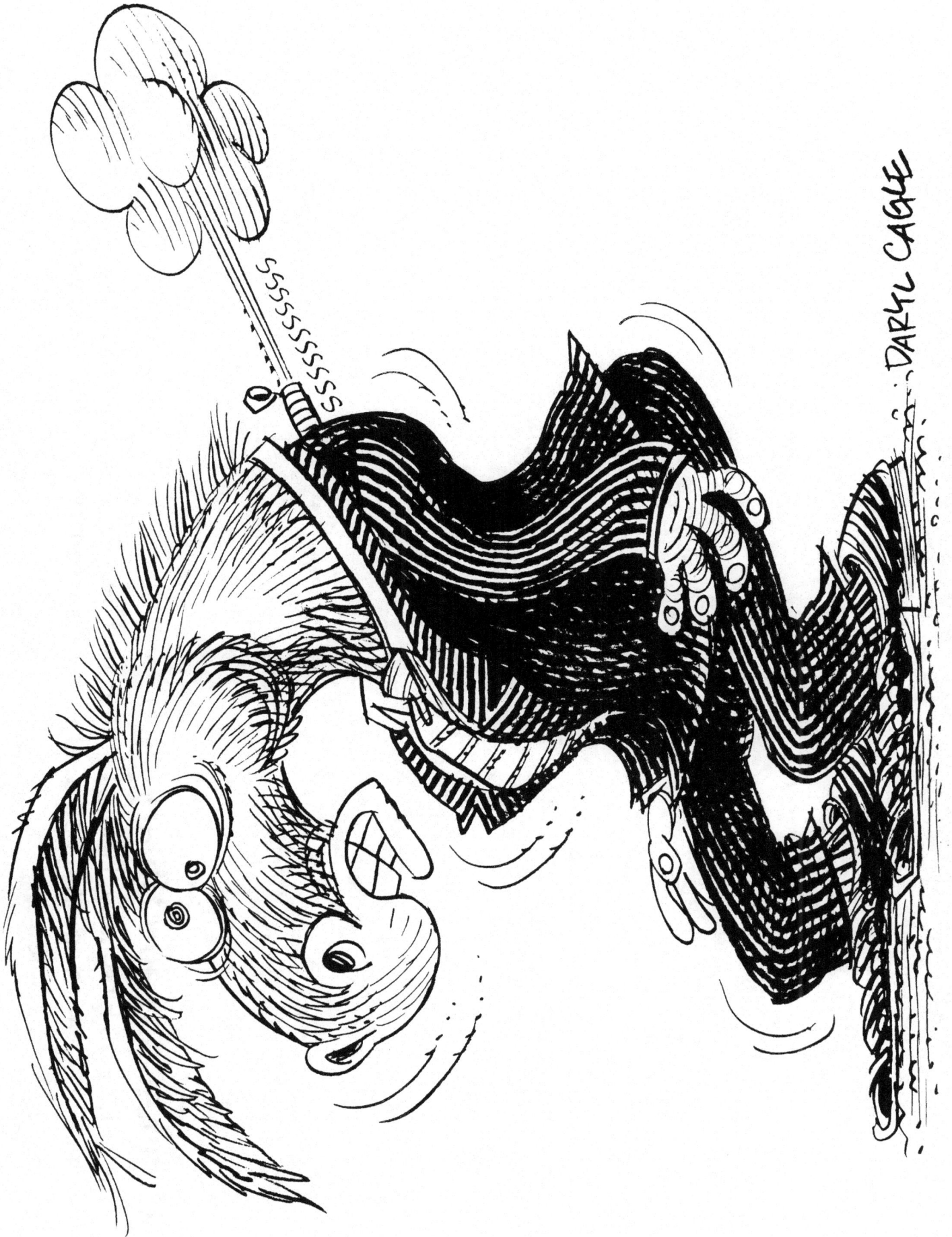

SSSSSSSSSS

DARYL CAGLE

ObamaCare and HillaryCare

When she was First Lady, Hillary championed healthcare reform. Her plan was better than ObamaCare, which smelled bad after many compromises in Congress. Now Hillary supports ObamaCare.

Hillary in 2008

Hillary thought she would run away with the 2008 election, instead, she ran off a cliff.

MEEP. MEEP.

DARYL CAGLE

Obama Played a "Smarter Game" in 2008

Now Hillary's campaign worries about being out-maneuvered by Trump.

The Two Most Unpopular Candidates Ever?

It looks like the angry, raucous 2016 Presidential race will feature the two most unpopular candidates ever.

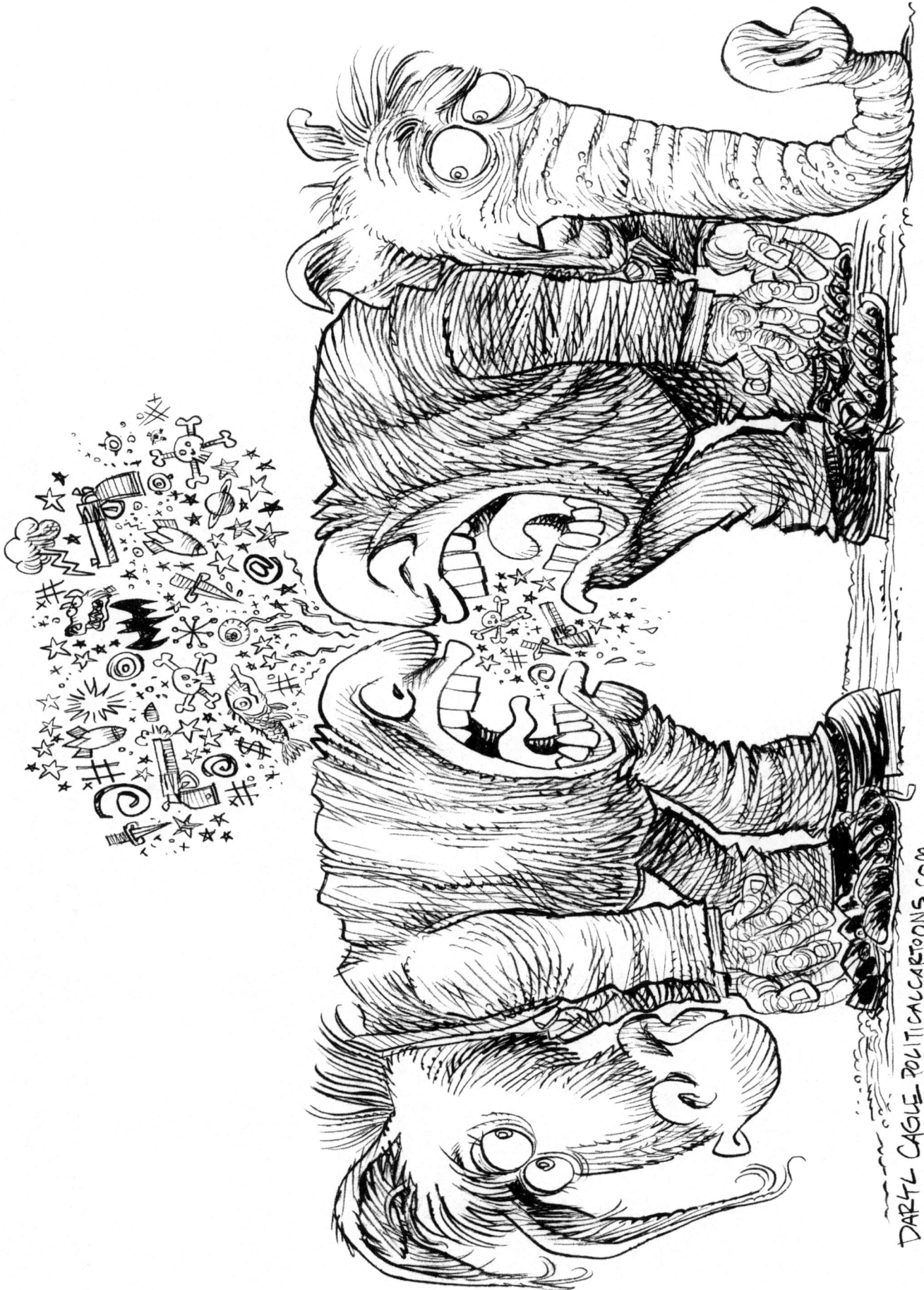

Hillary's Attack Dog, Bill

Just like in 2008, Bill Clinton is on Hillary's leash, ready to attack.

DARYL
CAGLE

Book Tours!

While they were out of office, Bill and Hillary both wrote books.

Living History
Hillary Rodham Clinton

BILL'S BOOK

DARYL CAGLE

Bill Clinton's "Operation"

Bill Clinton is a new man after his heart operation and a new diet that has changed his chubby personality to skinny.

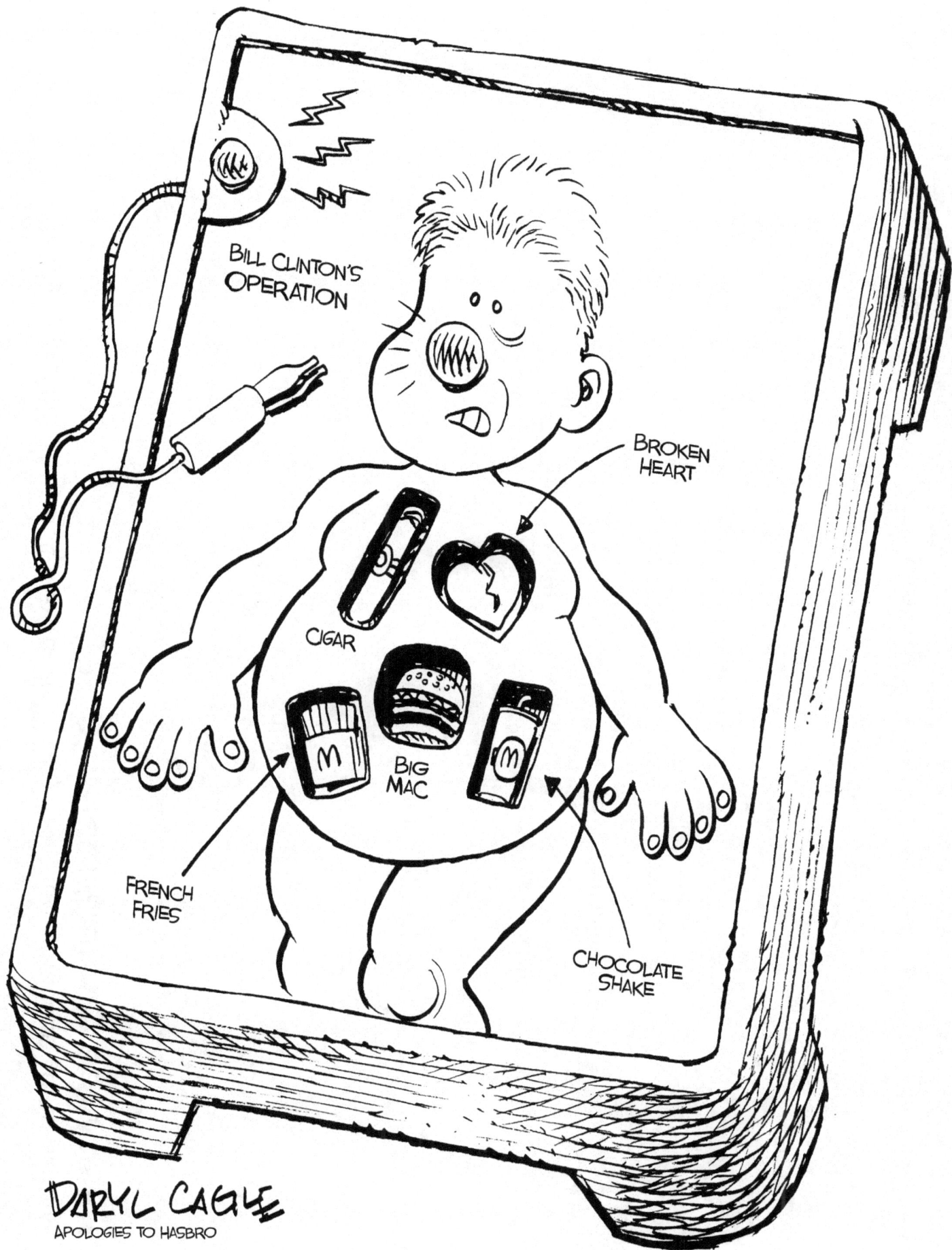

Hillary the Commander-in-Chief

With so many accomplishments, Hillary will make a fine Commander-in-Chief.

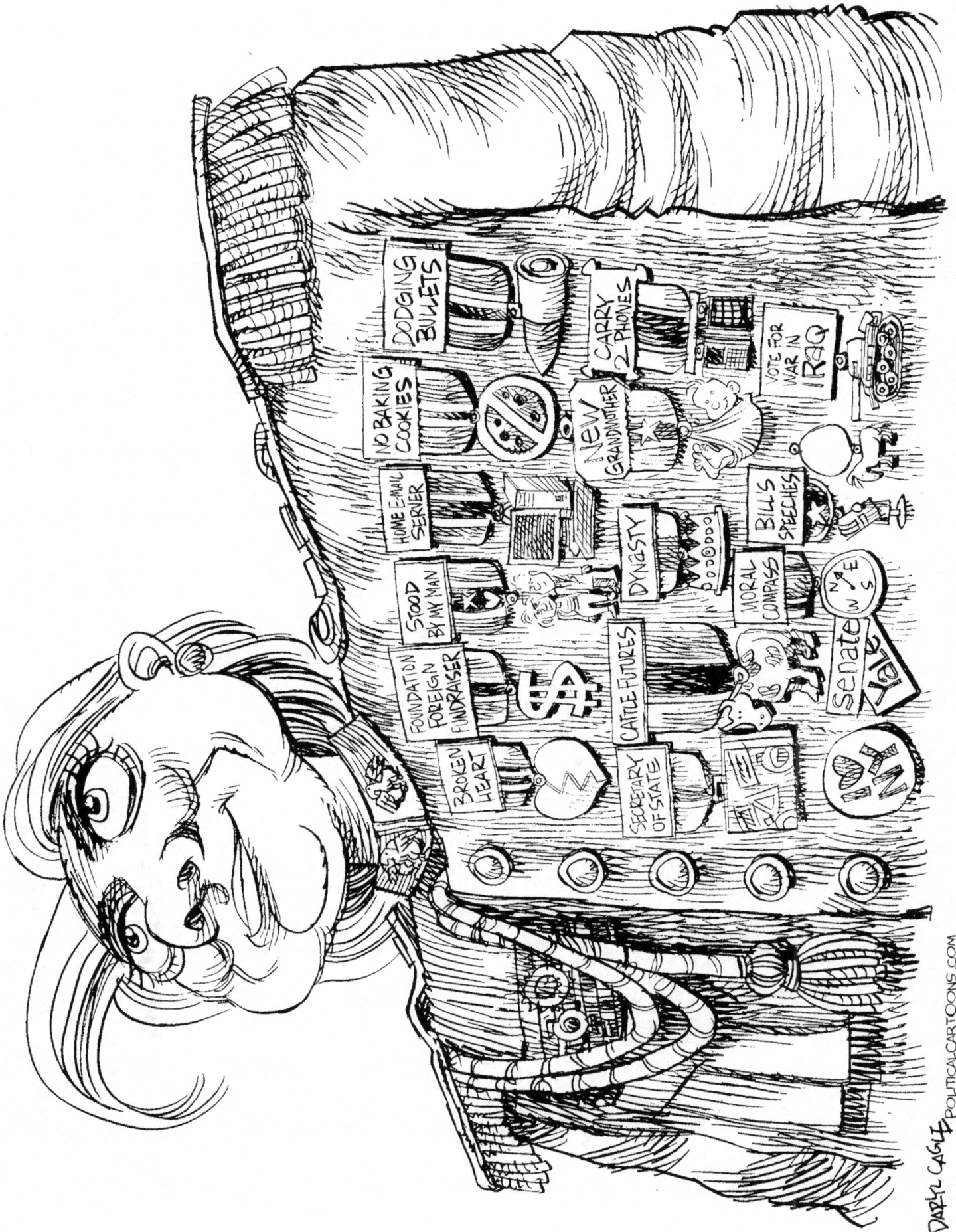

Fighting Democrats

Democrats hope that a strong performance by Hillary will carry over to other races, giving Dems the chance to win the Senate. It may be easy to forget that last time the Democrats controlled Congress they just fought among themselves.

For the past 35 years, Daryl Cagle has been one of America's most prolific cartoonists. He worked for 15 years with Jim Henson's Muppets, illustrating scores of books, magazines, calendars, and all manner of products. Daryl still sees pigs, frogs, Sesame Street and Fraggle Rock characters when he closes his eyes. He worked as the editorial cartoonist in Hawaii, then was the cartoonist for the Washington Post's Slate.com site and msnbc.com. Daryl is America's most widely syndicated editorial cartoonist.

To see more of Daryl's work visit DarylCagle.com. To reprint cartoons from Daryl and from the top editorial cartoonists around the world, visit PoliticalCartoons.com or call (805) 969-2829.

Collect All of the Daryl Cagle Coloring Books at CagleBook.com

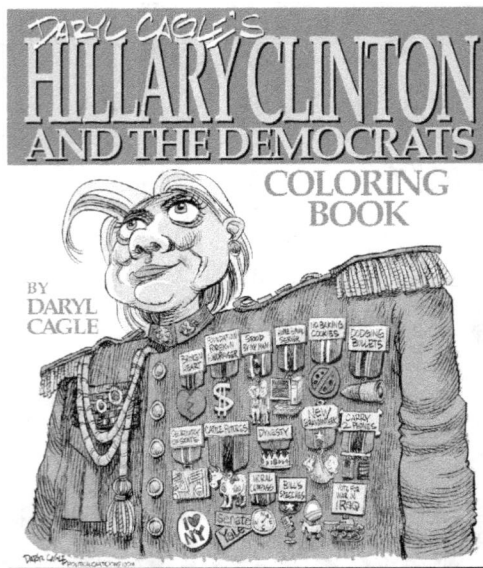

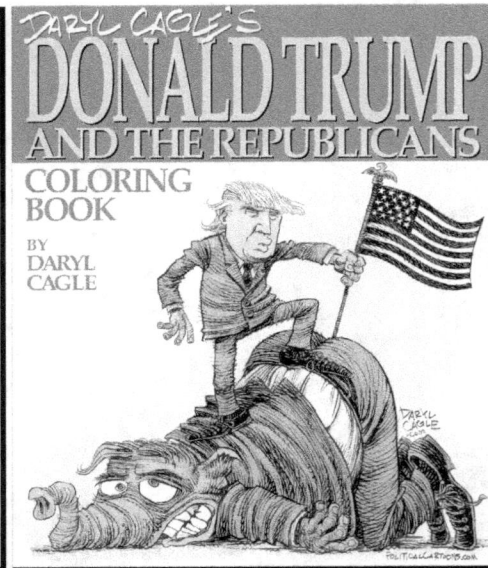

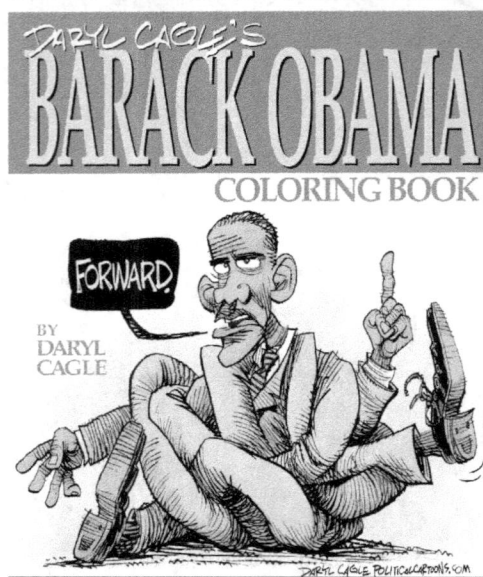

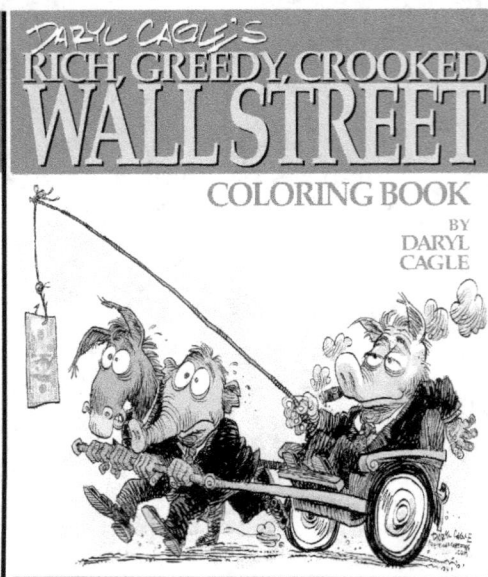

www.ingramcontent.com/pod-product-compliance
Lightning Source LLC
LaVergne TN
LVHW081349060426
835508LV00017B/1493